MW00472338

Partners in Prayer Advent 2017

s**ee**ING
a DIFFERENT
WORLD

ELIZABETH HAGAN

chalice
press

Saint Louis, Missouri

An imprint of Christian Board of Publication

Print: 9780827231511

EPDF (read-only): 9780827231535   EPUB: 9780827231528

ABOUT THE AUTHOR

Elizabeth Hagan is an ordained minister endorsed by the American Baptists and Disciples of Christ living in the Washington, D.C. area with her husband, Kevin, and daughter, Amelia. She is the author of *Birthed: Finding Grace through Infertility* and a frequent blogger at "Preacher on the Plaza." She's also the founder of Our Courageous Kids, a foundation seeking to help children growing up in international orphanages be able to go to college or secondary school. You can read more about her at elizabethhagan.com.

Candlelighting services available at ChalicePress.com

Spend a little family or private time in worship this Advent.
Go to ChalicePress.com, search for or click on
Partners in Prayer 2017, and follow the link to
free, downloadable candlelighting services.

Dear Reader,

Advent is a time in the church year that asks us to slow down, to avoid rushing on to the new calendar year so quickly. Advent calls us to consider again who we are as people of faith and what God is calling us to do.

Last year, as I preached an Advent series that kept me in the Old Testament until Christmas Eve, I felt convicted by Advent's call to action. Though we know the story ends as we celebrate Christ's birth in a few short days, Advent is an active season. It's a time when God longs for us to see what this world can become, and then join God in our shared creative calling.

I've found the wisdom and prophetic scriptures to be great teachers for Advent. They aren't afraid to turn everything we think we know upside down and say to us, "Look at this another way."

My hope for you, as you use *Partners in Prayer,* is that these devotions will be a tool in your own spiritual life. Over the next few weeks, you'll see the world through a different lens. You'll be spurred on by a different hope. You'll be comforted by a different peace. You'll be overflowing with a different joy; and you'll be treasuring a different love.

At the beginning of each week, you'll find quotes for reflection along with questions to think about during the week. I invite you to spend some time sitting with the introductory page before moving on to each Sunday's devotions.

I'm glad you've decided to take this intentional journey during Advent . It's a journey you're not making alone. If you'd like to continue to chat about any of these devotions, feel free to reach out to me over at elizabethhagan.com. I'd be glad to keep talking.

May Advent blessings abound,

Rev. Elizabeth

Seeing a Different Hope

"Hope is being able to see that there is light despite all of the darkness."

–Desmond Tutu

"Hope begins in the dark, the stubborn hope that if you just show up and try to do the right thing, the dawn will come. You wait and watch and work: you don't give up."

–Anne Lamott

Your reflections–

• What brings you the most hope right now?

• Where is God calling you to hope differently?

Read Isaiah 64:1–4

From ages past no one has heard,
  no ear has perceived,
no eye has seen any God besides you,
  who works for those who wait for him. (v. 4)

Here we are again, Advent. Opening ourselves to a time of expectation. Saying with our intentions that we want this season to be different. We want to wait in hope.

Isaiah has a lot to say about how hope is cultivated in waiting, and today's reading is no different. He reminds us that God appears in unlikely moments of our daily routines. In other words, get ready to be surprised!

But here's the thing about surprises. They can pass us by if we don't have eyes open to see them.

Last year I helped to plan a birthday party for a friend. For months good things were in the works all around him, yet he had no idea even until the last moment. When my friend pulled up to the party, he didn't see what was going on until he walked in the room and we exclaimed, "Happy birthday!" Only later did he feel the love that we had lived out for months while making our plans.

This Advent, don't wait until the big moment on Christmas Eve to hear the good news that Christ is born. This good news is available now. Open your eyes and see. Hope is here!

Pray with me:

Loving God, open our eyes to how the Spirit is already moving around us and wants to move in us even more. We want to wait with your vision for our lives and this world. AMEN.

Read Psalm 43:5

Why are you cast down, O my soul,
* and why are you disquieted within me?*
Hope in God; for I shall again praise him,
* my help and my God.*

This is the time of year when mailboxes fill up with Christmas cards. Some of these cards include Christmas letters.

Last year, after reading one Christmas letter, I couldn't help but think "This family must be closer to Jesus than ours!" Each of their children were excelling in school. Both parents were advancing in their careers. And they spend every Saturday morning volunteering at a local homeless shelter. I felt so deflated. Downcast, if you will.

Though we can get caught on the hamster wheel of jealousy any time of the year, it's much easier to do in December.

There's that other mother at our child's school, the one who bakes homemade cupcakes for the class party while we can barely make it to the grocery store . . .

There's that neighbor with the elaborate display of decorations in his front yard, and we haven't yet hung one ornament on our tree . . .

Or the friend on Facebook who . . .

And the list keeps going and going.

Yet Advent's hopeful pace calls us to measure success according to God's plans for us, not someone else's. It's a way of life that asks us to remember *who* we are hoping in. God is our help alone.

Pray with me:

God, we come to you with our weariness, our jealousies, and those places in our lives that make us feel "less than." Remind us that hope comes not from our striving to do better, but resides in you, and you alone. AMEN.

Read Jeremiah 29:11–14

For surely I know the plans I have for you, says the Lord, plans for your welfare and not for harm, to give you a future with hope. (v. 11)

Walk into any Christian bookstore in America and you'll find artwork, decorations, or coffee mugs with these verses printed on them (hey, this might be you!). Research any scripture memorization program for children and you'll find these verses on the list. Ask any regular church attender what his or her favorite scriptures are, and Jeremiah 29 will be among them.

We love these words because of the comfort of God's presence with us, and for the promise that something better is on the way.

But the original hearers of these prophetic words from Jeremiah were a community, not a singular person, as we often interpret them. As Israel sought to make sense of its time of exile in Babylon, Jeremiah wanted to infuse hope within them. They would not be in exile forever. God would take them home, together.

The same is true for us. Our collective calling is also to this restorative work—bringing hope to members of our community who feel stuck in exile with no way out:

- Single mothers who don't have funds to buy Christmas gifts for their kids

- Men and women living on death row for crimes they did not commit

- Families crying tears of grief and anger every night because an act of gun violence took a child away

How can we usher in God's good plans for them?

Will you pray with me?

God, we're hoping in you today. Hoping not just for ourselves, but for all those in our community who need fresh strokes of your grace. Help us to speak your hope and be your hope to those who feel forgotten around us. AMEN.

Read Isaiah 43:18–21

Do not remember the former things,
*   or consider the things of old.*
I am about to do a new thing;
*   now it springs forth, do you not perceive it? (vv. 18–19)*

As we tend to the work of seeing hope differently, we can easily encounter roadblocks. It's that pesky friend called our past. If your past is anything like mine, it likes to tell you stories.

Stories like, "When you tried to start that new program at church last year, remember, no one came."

Stories like, "The last time you made a huge career move, it was such a flop."

Stories like, "Last Christmas at the dinner table, you took a stand against racism. You can count the people who haven't spoken with you since!"

As we listen to these voices, we stop the God-given dream within us before it even starts. Yet Advent reminds us that the way things have always been done simply won't work anymore in God's kingdom. We must lay the past to rest. God is about to do a new thing; now it springs forth. Do we perceive it?"

Today, sit with this: God's hope always leads us toward the future a place where the unimaginable is possible. Our God is a God who makes the way through the wilderness. Our God is a God who tames the wild beasts. Our God is a God who gives water in the dry places. Our God *can* make all things new.

Will you pray with me?

Ever-present God, we don't want to be paralyzed by roadblocks. We want to live into your new things—whatever they may be for us. Surround us with teachers who call us out when we feel like going back to the wilderness. AMEN.

Read Lamentations 3:21–23

But this I call to mind,
*   and therefore I have hope:*
The steadfast love of the LORD never ceases,
*   his mercies never come to an end;*
they are new every morning;
*   great is your faithfulness.*

Hope, as much as we cling to it, can easily get lost in our lives. Setbacks come. Plans fall short. But the writer of Lamentations encourages us to give hope's work in us another chance. Why? Because "the steadfast love of the LORD never ceases." Love can give us a different hope.

For many years, I dreamt of publishing a book about the long and difficult years waiting for a child to enter our family. But as much as I found the courage to share our infertility story with the world, personal and emotional setbacks kept me from my goal. At one point, I completely gave up. I put the manuscript on the shelf. I thought I was done.

Yet, such is not the end of the story. I did publish *Birthed: Finding Grace Through Infertility* last December with Chalice Press. I was able to do this because of those who loved it out of me. Friends who came alongside me and said, "The world needs this story. And they need it from you." Friends who pushed me with compassion and wouldn't let me quit until it was finished.

Moments like this are what the exclamation "Great is thy faithfulness!" is all about. Love shows up in community. Love gives us everything we need to see hope differently.

Will you pray with me?

Sometimes, God, we've quit. We've let fear write the pages of our stories. When we find ourselves in that place, send love our way. AMEN.

Read Proverbs 13:12

Hope deferred makes the heart sick,
but a desire fulfilled is a tree of life.

The book of Proverbs is the original "worst case survival" handbook. Yet it's full of so much wisdom that it's easy to get lost in if you read too much in one sitting.

I remember the day I was first introduced to today's verse. I was sitting on a plane next to a friend as she was preparing to lead a study at her church. She stopped for a moment and handed me her Bible with her finger on this verse. Together we just sat in silence for a moment. For my friend knew:

I was struggling to find my footing in my career.

I was anxious about a situation my husband faced at work.

I was worried for a mutual friend who thought she'd beaten cancer, only to realize chemotherapy was in the cards *again*.

Worst of all, no matter what I did to bring new direction, comfort, and hope, nothing changed.

Now I realize what my wise friend wanted me to see that day: new hope. A time would come when my desires would be fulfilled. Maybe not in the ways I wanted. But hope asked me to wait with openness.

Such is the work of Advent even during these shorter days of sunlight. We preach the good news that indeed our waiting gives our roots strength; roots that one day will grow a strong tree, full of life.

Will you pray with me?

Faithful God, sometimes we don't feel your faithfulness. Our hearts are sick. But this is not the full story. You invite us to take the long view, to see how a "no" today is not a "no" forever. Help us lean in that direction right now. AMEN.

Read Isaiah 32:1–5

Then the eyes of those who have sight will not be closed,
*   and the ears of those who have hearing will listen.*
The minds of the rash will have good judgment,
*   and the tongues of stammerers will speak readily and distinctly.*
*   (vv. 3–4)*

The texts of Advent, this one included, remind us that all is not as it should be in this world.

Those appointed to rule over us don't always lead with righteousness. The wrong people are exalted. We forget the sick, the imprisoned, and the lonely. The rich get richer.

But as much as Isaiah's words tell us what is not right in the world, they also help us see differently. What is will not always be! Why? God wants *US* to be part of the change: to open eyes, to invite ears to listen to new conversations, and to open our mouths in ways that include others.

A friend of mine leads a nonprofit organization dedicated to ending homelessness. Her faith compels her to use her education, intellect, and God-given courage to speak for those caught in endless cycles of poverty. Many call the goal of her work unattainable. Yet she's quick to fire back: "If we don't believe in and work toward the empowerment of all people, who will?" Her advocacy shines a bright light into the new world that God wants to create.

It would be easy to write off hope in action as a pie-in-the-sky dream, saying, "Well, that's nice but it's never going to happen." But as people of faith, God gave us this work!

Will you pray with me?

Loving God, give us clear vision to see beyond what is, to what can be. Help our steps be aligned with your dreams for all our brothers and sisters. Embolden us with courage as we act! AMEN.

Seeing a Different Peace

"If we have no peace, it is because we have forgotten that we belong to each other."

–Mother Teresa

"God's dream for us is not simply peace of mind, but peace on earth."

–Marcus Borg

Your reflections–

• What brings you the most peace right now?

• How is God calling you to work for peace differently?

Read Isaiah 40:1–11

A voice cries out:
*"In the wilderness prepare the way of the L*ORD,
make straight in the desert a highway for our God." (v. 3)

When I think about the times in my life when "peace" was *not* a word that described my demeanor, the reason had everything to do with *where* my confidence lay.

Was my peace for the future dependent on my own ability to get a job, or in the One who said I'd never be left alone or deserted?

Was my peace about my relationship status grounded in my communication skills and likability, or in the One who knew I needed companionship?

Was my peace for the future of my country tied to human ability to change, or to the One who called himself the Prince of Peace?

Our Isaiah reading offers us the chance to see peace differently. God asks us to lay aside what we think we can do, and experience the comfort of who God already is. God invites us to remember that no matter how gifted we think we are, at the end of our days we're just like the grass that withers and the flower that fades. True peace comes when we remember we're not in control and never will be. Surrender gives us this beautiful gift.

Will you pray with me?

God of peace, we forget that you are the author of our days. We seek peace in people, things, and goals that do not satisfy. Reboot our lives this day and give us true peace. AMEN.

Read Jeremiah 6:13–16

Thus says the LORD:
Stand at the crossroads, and look, and ask for the ancient paths,
where the good way lies; and walk in it,
*   and find rest for your souls.*
But they said, "We will not walk in it." (v. 16)

"What a Friend We Have in Jesus" is a hymn many of us sing often in church. When I sang it recently, I found my mind stuck on these words:

"O what peace we often forfeit, O what needless pain we bear, all because we do not carry everything to God in prayer."

I felt convicted on the spot for the times I have tried to "go it alone" without remembering God is present. For God wants to carry my burdens. God longs to give me direction about what to do next.

As Jeremiah writes to a people soon to be under attack, he offers them a choice. Place your confidence in human leaders who readily seek to deceive you, or ask God for guidance. The prophet reminds us that if we draw upon the wisdom of God, we'll find rest for our souls.

Doesn't that sound nice in the middle of December? *Rest.*

Then let us pray. Not just the short prayer at the end of this devotion, but a full day of prayer. A day of remembering we belong to God. A day of turning over our worries to God. Here, we will find rest for our souls.

Will you pray with me?

God of peace, we invite you into our day all the nooks and crannies of it. The stuff we don't want you to see, and the stuff we do. The moments when we feel alive, and the moments when we fill with fear. We want to walk with you all day long. AMEN.

Read Psalm 85:8–13

Let me hear what God the LORD will speak,
for he will speak peace to his people,
to his faithful, to those who turn to him in their hearts. (v. 8)

If you were to describe your personal experience of God, what words would you use?

Some of you might speak of God's holiness, for you've seen God do miracles in your life that are beyond all comprehension.

Some of you might speak about God's love, for no matter what you've been through in your life, you've never felt God has left you.

Some of you might describe God's judgment, for rarely are you separated from guilt when you make a less-than-perfect decision.

My answer would be the latter. Growing up in my church, I heard a lot more about God's judgment than I ever did about God's love. My teachers said God had many rules, and if I didn't follow God's rules, I was not as good as those who did. What pressure and anxiety this produced. Anxiety, as we know, is not a state of peace.

If you find yourself buried in guilt or judgment today, Psalm 85 invites you to re-see. It invites us to see God through the lens of love, not just for ourselves, but for our neighbors and the entire created world too. The Lord, we are told, longs to give us what is good. God wants us not only to work for peace, but to be at peace.

Will you pray with me?

Loving God, you long for our bodies, our families, and our neighbors to be at peace. You long for us to see you rightly, as the giver of all good gifts. Surround us with NEW vision for our lives today, for we want to see you as you are! AMEN.

Read Isaiah 11:1–9

The wolf shall live with the lamb,
  the leopard shall lie down with the kid,
the calf and the lion and the fatling together. (v. 6)

Isaiah 11 paints a picture with vivid words about seeing peace differently. Though it sounds like a fairy tale, the lion lying down with the lamb and the cow and bear grazing together, it's not. God wants to show us a new way to live in this world. God is offering us new life, not only in the paradoxical places but in the possibilities around us that seem dead and gone. God moves in situations that may feel dead to us.

But where is this?

Some in our modern context would say we can find God at work in who is elected to office. Or those who find their way into Oprah's Book Club list. Or in the social media voices with the most retweets and likes.

But Isaiah 11 would beg us to turn away from all this and go to the stumps.

Isaiah would tell us to start with the deadest of dead ministries. The deadest of dead dreams. The deadest of dead relationships. There, God is at work. Peace springs up among the ashes.

In what dead thing in your life does God want to work today?

Will you pray with me?

Resurrecting God, take us to the stumps of our stories. Take us to the dead places within our lives and this world. Remind us that here, you long to do something new. AMEN.

Read Jeremiah 29:7

"Also, seek the peace and prosperity of the city to which I have carried you into exile. Pray to the LORD for it, because if it prospers, you too will prosper." (NIV)

It's easy to believe that peace looks like perfection. The right place. The right time. The right people all living together in harmony.

Many of us use this definition of peace to justify why we don't act. When it's the right time, we say, we will.

But Jeremiah's exhortation to the nation of Israel dispels this practice. He encouraged his first hearers to seek the "peace" of the city where they were, even if it was not where they wanted to be.

And by peace, I don't believe he's talking about contentment. Or being a doormat to injustice. I believe he's talking about the peace of human-to-human connection: seeing people, loving people, right where you are.

Several years ago, I found myself living in a city I did not want to live in. I had a horrible attitude about it. I exuded negative energy. And as much as I said that I wanted to make peace with my circumstances, I never did. Instead, I isolated myself. My heart wasn't open to seeing my neighbors. I wished I could move back home.

But slowly, thanks to a lot of grace and some new friends, my attitude changed, and I learned this lesson: when you pray for your surroundings to prosper, there's hope for you to prosper in them.

Will you pray with me?

Loving God, it's easy to make faith such a personal matter that we forget our faith is always communal. No matter if we love the place where we are right now or can't wait to get out of town, teach us to pray for the prosperity of all the people around us. AMEN.

Read Isaiah 42:14

For a long time I have held my peace,
I have kept still and restrained myself;
now I will cry out like a woman in labor,
I will gasp and pant.

I don't know if your family is anything like mine, but around the holidays especially, certain topics must be avoided in order to keep the peace.

Casseroles, turkey, and sweet potato pie do not go well with politics or religion, it seems. If you are like me, you make the choice to keep the peace out of respect for your elders. Or to be invited back next year. Or at least to make it to January 2018 without World War III erupting in your living room.

But Isaiah's words remind us that there comes a point in our life of faith when we can't be silent. We must let our voices be heard. Not because of our ego or a desire to be right, but because the presence of God in our life compels us to speak. Like a woman in labor, we must give birth to something new.

Here's the thing: peace is not about keeping everyone happy (as much as we wish it was). Living in peace is about authenticity. It's about going to bed at night knowing you've fully shown up for the day. It's about having the courage to be who you are without shame. When we do this, we give others permission to do the same.

Will you pray with me?

God, help us to be peacemakers this week. Fill us up with courage to be the people you've made us to be. Strengthen our hearts to walk in your paths. Give us patience with others who have not yet learned to cry out. For truly, we're all in the birthing room together. AMEN.

Read Isaiah 43:1–7

Do not fear, for I have redeemed you;
I have called you by name, you are mine.
When you pass through the waters, I will be with you. (vv. 1b–2a)

These words from Isaiah are often read at funerals. When folks are gathered to mourn a loss, it seems important to remind them that God is there. God has not forgotten them. God is with their loved ones in this very dark hour.

But I don't think Isaiah's words are exclusive to funeral goers. They are words for any of us who've lost sight of our identity.

We're reminded that in the family of God, we belong.

We're reminded that in the family of God, we are loved.

We're reminded that in the family of God, we are known individually by the Creator of the Universe.

It's a timeless message, but one that is part of the NEW that God longs to give our world. Can you imagine how we might live if we truly believed we belong, we are loved, and we are known by God?

This, my friends, is the invitation to the new peace with which God is longing to fill our world this Advent. It's a gift of being enough. It's a gift of knowing we're okay (even when life is not). And it's a gift of peace beyond our circumstances. We shall not be moved.

Will you pray with me?

Loving God, we forget so easily our place as your beloveds. Come Holy Spirit, come into this day and remind us of our place in the order of things, that most of all we are seen and heard by you. AMEN.

Seeing a Different Joy

"Joy does not simply happen to us. We have to choose joy and keep choosing joy every day."

–Henri J.M. Nouwen

"Joy comes to us in ordinary moments. We risk missing out when we get too busy chasing down the extraordinary."

–Brené Brown

Your reflections–

• What brings you the most joy right now?

• Where is God calling you to see joy differently?

Read Isaiah 61:1–4

The spirit of the Lord GOD is upon me,
because the LORD has anointed me;
he has sent me to bring good news to the oppressed,
to bind up the brokenhearted. (v.1)

A friend was telling me recently about the present she received from her parents on her 16th birthday. They bought her a car. Even though it was a used clunker, she was in shock. As the oldest of four children, she knew her parents didn't have a lot of money. So what joy beamed from her face as she turned the keys in the ignition.

But then, before she could pull out of the driveway, her father told her, "Now, wait darling. You need to understand we bought you this because we want you to take your siblings to school."

Likewise, in this reading from Isaiah, we find a message about a joy that is meant to be shared.

As the Hebrew people return from exile in Babylon and discern that their homeland is not exactly as they imagined it, Isaiah is calling them to see new joy.

This text asks us all: "Do you want to know joy?" If we do, Isaiah responds, go to the place where folks are most oppressed, brokenhearted, and in bondage, and be a light of God's presence. Show God's favor. Share!

It's quite a temptation this time of year to be consumed with our family, our presents, and our interests. But the calling of Advent always leads us out to share good news.

Will you pray with me?

God, you've given us joy so that we can share it. As we move through this day, help us to see those who need some good news. Give us courage, then, to be bearers of joy. AMEN.

Read Psalm 30:4–5

Weeping may linger for the night,
but joy comes with the morning. (v. 5b)

Joy is not always an emotion we feel. Life can be so hard in this broken landscape of ours. Illnesses come out of nowhere. Marriages end sooner than we would like. Friendships fizzle. Pay cuts come at work. We read the latest headlines and wonder how we are going to make it out of bed in the morning *again*.

But a spiritual perspective on life asks us to make room for joy, no matter what is going on in the world or in our home. The Psalmist invites us to see joy. We are promised that joy will return, even if we don't feel it now.

The underlying question of Psalm 30 is whether or not we believe God is good. If we do believe this, then joy is possible. God's justice will prevail in the end–although we might be asked to linger in the darkness longer than we would like.

In response to this promise of coming redemption, God asks us to worship. God asks us to keep singing. God asks us to lift our heads. God asks us to turn our gaze from our circumstances toward the mystery of the Divine, the direction where joy reigns.

Will you pray with me?

Good God, we thank you for being present in the hardest places of our journey, giving us joy to see what a beautiful tapestry you are weaving for all that is to come. Today, we may or may not be joyful, but we can proclaim your goodness even still. AMEN.

Read Psalm 51:10–12

Restore to me the joy of your salvation,
and sustain in me a willing spirit. (v. 12)

Many of us have a hard time talking about sin, even in church. For the word "sin" is often used to label some people as "bad" and others as "good." Or it's used to place harsh judgment on our choices, or the choices of those we love. We who believe God is love, and who don't want to be "that kind of Christian," avoid talking about sin.

However, as a pastor, I don't know how to talk about God's good news without talking about sin. Sin robs us of God's best. Sin takes from us the delight of being a human, made in the image of our Creator. Sin deprives us of joy.

King David, in his famous confessional psalm, speaks of how sin has led him on a joyless path. He speaks to God bluntly, saying that after having an affair with Bathsheba, lying about it, and scheming to arrange the death of her husband, his actions brought him regret. Not joy.

David asks God to not let sin be the end of his story. "Give me a fresh start. Put my feet on a new journey. I want to know joy again."

Here's the beauty of it all—restarts are always possible. God's grace abounds. Joy can always return. We just need to ask.

Will you pray with me?

Loving God, we want to taste more of your joy. We want our cups to brim in delight with what it means to be alive. Today, open our eyes to those joy-zapping parts of our lives. Teach us to confess our sin. AMEN.

Read Isaiah 35:5–10

And the ransomed of the Lord shall return,
*   and come to Zion with singing;*
everlasting joy shall be upon their heads. (v. 10a)

When I was six years old, our family experienced a Christmas I will never forget. Thanks to a distant family member who owned a toy company, a heap of toys made its way to our living room. Dolls in every color, shape, and size. Train sets. Play houses. Coloring books. Bouncing balls. You name it, we had it. I couldn't wait to play with it all.

But before I got very far with my plans, my mother said it wasn't for me. "What?"

She said we would give these toys to several area churches hosting drives for the homeless and for out-of-work parents. Soon pastors would be coming to our house to pick up boxes. I could only pick one thing. We'd share the rest.

Though filled with disappointment, I learned an important lesson that day about joy. In God's family, we share. When one of us receives a blessing, it's not so we can brag about our bounty, but so others can know love too.

Isaiah echoes this truth as he describes the new world God longs to create. He carefully selects plural pronouns to speak about joy, reminding us that our path moving forward is not a path for us alone. It's a path to travel together. Joy comes always in sharing.

Will you pray with me?

God, thank you for inviting us to be co-creators with you. When we are tempted to hoard our blessings, remind us that joy always comes in giving. We want to love as you first loved us. AMEN.

Read Jeremiah 15:16

Your words were found, and I ate them,
and your words became to me a joy
and the delight of my heart;
for I am called by your name,
O LORD, God of hosts.

As Christmas nears, we might feel weariness as we light the candle of joy. Our to-do lists are long. Our extra stashes of cash are shrinking. Our children are hyped up on sugar and Santa and no longer in school. Many of us just want a long Christmas nap, though it's still days away.

This reading from Jeremiah brings us back to Advent. Jeremiah receives encouragement to journey back to the center—back to joy—and offers the same invitation: "Your words became to me a joy."

The phrase "your words" is an image straight from the call of Jeremiah in chapter 1. The Lord comes to a young Jeremiah, reaches out, and puts words in Jeremiah's mouth. Jeremiah takes on the responsibility of being God's mouthpiece to a community of people his life's purpose.

In the same way, our joy comes from living our life's purpose: knowing God, loving God, and serving God wherever we find our feet planted today.

Let us not get so distracted by the things around us that we miss God's invitation. Our to-do lists often become dramatically shorter when we let go of the stuff that is not part of God's best for us.

Will you pray with me?

God who calls us all by name, we are grateful for your lavish love. Thank you for seeking us out just as you did with your prophets long ago. Help us to take in your word today so that we don't get distracted by all the tasks that aren't meant for our attention. AMEN.

Read Proverbs 14:10

The heart knows its own bitterness,
and no stranger shares its joy.

How many times have you heard the phrase, "If you don't have anything nice to say about someone, don't say anything at all." (And then immediately gone back to not following this advice).

It can feel so good to gripe about how we weren't given our fair share of opportunities at work. It can feel so good to complain about how our life partner is not supporting us. It can feel so good to speak negative words about the way our friends choose to parent their children.

Yet each time you and I choose to speak negatively, we open the door to bitterness. The resentment over what we think we should have, but don't, can leave an unpleasant trail. Especially during a season brimming with expectations, it's easy for disappointment to creep in and ruin goodness quickly.

The writer of this proverb warns us of all of this. When joy *does* find its way into our lives, we're also less likely to share it. A bitter heart does not know how to make the transition into joy. For ultimately, joy is a communal emotion.

Spend some time today seeing how joy can flow from your life. What old grudges or ongoing disagreements do you need to release so that you can reflect more of God's goodness in the world?

Will you pray with me?

God, open up the bitter corners of our souls. Where are those places within us that need to receive a fresh wind of your Spirit? Give us the courage to move toward joy anew. AMEN.

Read Isaiah 61:8–11

*I will greatly rejoice in the L*ORD,
my whole being shall exult in my God;
for he has clothed me with the garments of salvation. (v. 10a)

How comfortable do you feel telling others about what God has done in your life? Is it something that comes naturally to you, or are you more private about your faith?

Every Sunday, the people in my home church gather 20 minutes before the service is scheduled to begin. Members and visitors alike are invited to stand up and share how God has been with them over the past week. Newcomers often comment on how intimidating this practice is—some even come to church late just to avoid it. But over time it grows on them. For as they hear the stories of how God is at work in others' lives, they sense the same in their own. It's amazing to me that every time I return, folks I wouldn't expect to share are sharing. Testimony seems to give birth to more testimony.

This portion of Isaiah encourages such a practice—the simple act of giving praise to God for what God has done in your life. Isaiah testifies that the Lord has given him salvation. The Lord has given the great gift of salvation! And he can't be silent! The act of testimony moves him in praise, so that all the world can see. Joy finds wings in his words.

Will you pray with me?

God, there's so much joy waiting to bubble up and overflow from within us. Give us the courage to speak when you call us to give testimony. AMEN.

Seeing a Different Love

"New life starts in the dark. Whether it is a seed in the ground, a baby in the womb, or Jesus in the tomb, it starts in the dark."

–Barbara Brown Taylor

"Instructions for living a life: Pay attention. Be astonished. Tell about it."

–Mary Oliver

Your reflections–

• What brings your life the most love right now?

• Where is God calling you to love differently?

Read Isaiah 9:2–7

The people who walked in darkness
have seen a great light;
those who lived in a land of deep darkness—
on them light has shined. (v. 2)

There's a huge difference between the posture of waiting and the posture of celebrating. When all our energy has gone into planning, preparing, and thinking about what life will be like when our blessing comes, often we don't have eyes to see its arrival.

In our reading for Christmas Eve, Isaiah invites us to begin celebrating. The light is here.

Last December, I got the chance of a lifetime. My husband and I were invited to a White House Christmas party. After we made our way through security, the ushers announced that the President and his wife would be walking down the stairs in front of us. I was so happy to have picked a great spot. But what did I do next? I got out my phone and snapped photo after photo, only to look up and realize I never saw the President. I missed my chance.

In the same way, our calling today is simple—to not let this moment pass by without seeing. It's easy to have our heads in the clouds, thinking about dinner tomorrow or trips to Grandma's or presents under the tree. But this is the moment to KNOW: the light is here. Love will soon be born. Let us see!

Will you pray with me?

God born on this night, we welcome you. We welcome you into our homes. We welcome you to our tables. We welcome you into our hearts. Help us know how to love you well. AMEN.

Read Luke 2:1–20

*But Mary treasured all these words and pondered them in her heart.
(v. 19)*

All Advent long, we've stuck close to prophetic and wisdom texts–texts that have expanded our vision of what life in the kingdom of God looks like. But today, everything has changed. On Christmas, we celebrate Love's presence among us. The second act of our story has begun. By the second chapter of Luke, we understand who will be the main character. Christ is born.

Verse 19 is one of my favorite parts of the Christmas story. After a long journey, a painful birth in a strange place, and the arrival of some worshipers, Luke gives us a vision of Mary. She's taking a step back. She's not letting the moments of this brilliant day pass without treasuring them. She's being fully present.

I wonder if the same could be said about us?

My invitation to you is to take on the practice of Mary. Reflect, renew, and rejoice! Find a quiet moment (or two) in this day–not in front of a TV or computer. In the quiet, simply be.

The call of the Christmas season will go on for many days. There will be time in those days to act on love. But for today, just bask in it. Treasure this gift of Jesus in your heart too.

Will you pray with me?

God who is Love with Us, draw us out of our own surroundings today to a place of quiet. Draw us to a place where we can remember that you are Love and you became Love so that we might know Love too. AMEN.

9780827203112
Ebooks also available

 When your one dream for life dies, how do you go on living? When infertility interrupted Elizabeth Hagan's plan to start a family, the path of grace offered her another way. Instead of giving birth to a child, she ended up birthing herself. Along the way, Hagan learned that you can't control how fast your dreams come true, if they come true at all, but you can find grace for embracing your life in the present tense, grief and all.

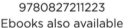